Alpaca Fleece –
What Can You Do
With It?

Annaliese Reis

DEDICATION

To my long suffering partner who encouraged me to write this book after I found the answers to "What can I do with all of this fleece?".

CONTENTS

ACKNOWLEDGEMENTS

Without the help and advice from so many, this book would never have been written. My thanks to you all for your patience and understanding in answering my never ending questions..

1 PREFACE

One of the reasons we had ventured into having Alpacas was because of the lovely fleece and the opportunities it offered us to use our creative talents. We were fortunate that we already had the land and outbuildings so that wasn't an issue. We didn't know much about Alpacas other than what they looked like but as fortune had it, we came across a knowledgeable breeder. Part of the purchase price included support, and we were able to quickly learn how to handle the alpacas, what to feed them on, as well as what injections and drenches they needed. Admittedly some of the learning took us quite by surprise for the idea of injections and drenches had never occurred to us. But we quickly got to grips with all that was required in the sure and certain knowledge that if we couldn't do it then the vet could.

We actually looked forward to shearing day with great excitement, although the day was a little scarred by the fact that the Alpacas didn't seem to enjoy it one little bit.

I remember thinking how much smaller the Alpacas looked after shearing – no longer the very large animals that had initially made me feel a little intimidated, but now the much smaller cuddlier animal that looked a little grateful for their instant weight loss and clearly now they would be a lot cooler.

But now came the shock – there was simply so much fleece from all of them! I had never dreamed of such a lot of fleece from one animal. It had never occurred to me that there would be so much to deal with – so now what! Well, the easiest option was to put all the sacks of fleece in the barn and that's just what I did.

I had always been led to believe that the fleeces were easily sold but to quote the film Field of Dreams 'and the people will come' it didn't happen – well not at a price that I was willing to accept. For me the selling price had to cover the shearing costs.

After many months of research and training, I finally found the answer to my repeated question of 'What Do I Do With All These Fleeces?

It's been a long journey but one that I wanted to share with all those people that have sacks full of fleece stored in their barn. That lovely fleece from your beautiful alpaca needs to be shared with others so that they too can appreciate the softness, the warmth, and the sheer cosiness of the fleece that your alpaca grew for you.

I hope that this book will fill you with enthusiasm taking you on a journey of discovery as you learn new crafts. But more importantly I hope it answers the question for you 'What Can I Do With My Alpaca fleeces?'

Annaliese Reis - August 2014

2 YOUR ALPACA INVESTMENT

Alpacas belong to the camelid family, and come in varying sizes and colours. Whilst there are six different kinds of camelids, the two we are used to seeing in Alpaca farming are the Huacaya with its dense crimpy alpaca fleece, and the rarer Suri with its elegant, silky fleece.

Prior to the European colonisation of the Americas, Alpacas were already highly prized. They were primarily used as a source of meat, but clothing and blankets were also made from the soft dense alpaca fleeces. Ensuring nothing was wasted, the hides were also used, and the manure was dried for fuel.

The Incas valued the Alpaca highly and in fact measured their own status and wealth by how much cloth they had, with most of it coming from the Alpaca.

Llamas and alpacas were central to the Incan religious and ritualistic practices and sadly they were used as sacrifices to honour the gods.

Nowadays there are varying reasons to keep Alpacas. Whilst some alpaca owners keep them purely as pets, they do make excellent guard animals for sheep and chickens as foxes will most certainly stay away whilst there is an alpaca in sight. Many owners also have holiday accommodation and use their Alpacas as an attraction for their paying guests. Some enthusiasts keep them purely for showing and winning the treasured sash and rosette. However, it seems that many alpaca owners view their herd as an investment for their future and become alpaca breeders with the main focus being to buy and sell alpacas in order to improve their investment.

Whatever the reason for your purchase, the one certain thing is that you will have to have the animal sheared every year and unless you have hoards of empty outbuildings, you have to do something with it.

It does sadden me the amount of people who simply chuck the fleeces in the barn and forget about them, making no attempt to monetise them or share their beauty. Commercially it doesn't make sense for there are shearing costs and you should at least try to recoup that money.

3 PREPARING FOR SHEARING

It's that time again and the shearer is coming in a few days and you have to prepare for the visit.

It's important that the area you have chosen for shearing is scrupulously clean. This is of course for two reasons – firstly you want to ensure that should your animal get cut during shearing, that he/she doesn't run the risk of getting an infection. Secondly you need to ensure that there is no organic matter or dust lying around that could cling onto your fleeces. The dust in the fleece could cause the shearer a problem by blunting his tools, and you want to avoid having to arduously remove organic matter from the fleeces before you pack them!

If the weather forecast is good then you have no problem. But if there is a risk of rain then you need to bring your animals into a dry area before it rains. Your shearer may refuse to shear them if they are wet, for it could damage his tools, but from your fleece point of view, you really don't want a wet fleece that will have to be dried before you can pack it away.

There are many methods of shearing and you need to liaise with your shearer as to how he needs the area set up before he arrives. Some shearers insist on all the alpacas being in the vicinity whilst some will fetch them from the fields for you. Personally I like to bring them in before the shearer arrives so that the whole operation can be conducted as soon as possible. Alpacas are sensitive animals and don't like to be restrained in an area for too long. They seem to work on the 100th Monkey Syndrome and can pass the message to each other that they are about to have an experience that they probably won't enjoy.

Do make sure that your shearer is experienced with Alpacas. They are not sheep, can't be manhandled like sheep, and shouldn't be shorn like sheep! I heard a story of an Alpaca shearer who was self taught – whilst he did restrain the animal securely he sheared them from hind foot across the blanket to the front foot. As he sheared his helper removed bits of the fleece, mixing blanket with legs and the owners just ended up with a pile of handfuls of fleece. The result was of course a ruined fleece, for no beautiful blanket to admire and a complete mix of blanket and legs. The animal though was a lot cooler so there was some sort of result.

Any good shearer will remove the blanket for you in virtually one piece so that you can pack it straight away. The remaining part of the fleece can then be easily collected and stored separately.

If you have helpers available this is a good time to skirt the blanket. Lay it out on a flat surface with the cut side facing up. This should be done on a wire mesh table (skirting table) that allows debris to fall from the fleece. Spend a little time looking over the edges of the fleece and remove debris and any obvious guard hairs (seen as straight coarse hairs), which would devalue the fleece's consistency. Fold the sides of the fleece into the middle and roll the fleece up gently.

How you store your fleece is a matter of personal choice. But you need to make sure that the fleeces are dry before storage. A wet fleece will eventually grow mould and taint the entire fleece making it completely unusable. We use paper feed bags or potato sacks that have several layers, for storage. This way the blanket goes in, the layer is folded over the fleece and then the remaining fleece is placed in and the next layer folded over it.

If your shearer allows you the time, it is a great opportunity to weigh your blanket and the separated fleece and write it on the outside of the bag for future use. If you are lucky you will have several helpers on hand, who could do this for you.

Incidentally, shearing time is a great time to have the teeth and toes dealt with, and to do any injections or drenching. Most shearers offer to do the teeth and toes and some to even do the injections for you. It does of course sometimes add to the shearing cost, but it does make life a lot easier when the Alpaca is in a restrained position.

If you are planning on having your fibre evaluated for micron count (histogram) then you should tell your shearer before he starts. He will take a small sample from the mid-side of the alpaca, which you then need to place in a ziplock bag to go off to your provider to make the appropriate measurements and send you a report.

4 ABOUT FIBRE

It is outside the remit of this book to delve into histogram reports, but suffice it to say that the report only reveals the findings of that piece of fleece on that day. If the sample is taken incorrectly (i.e. not close to the skin) it will give an inaccurate result. As the animal gets older, one can expect the micron count to increase.

So what purpose does the micron count serve? Whilst it is a useful tool for determining the health of your alpaca, it is also used for genetic improvement.

The fleece sample when analysed, records, amongst other things, the diameter of the fibres and this is expressed in microns (one millionth of a metre, or one thousandth of a millimetre). It is used by many to determine what usage will be made of the fleece, but this differs throughout the Alpaca Community and between mill spinners and hand spinners.

As a guideline only I detail some of the guidance I have been given from Alpaca owners both in the UK, and other countries. It does make the list a little confusing for each user appears to have different ideas of what micron to use for different things.

As I've said it's just a guideline.

Up to 20 microns – lightweight scarves (pashmina-type), shawls, vests

20-23 microns – worsted clothing, jackets, suits, medium weight knitting yarn

Up to 25 microns – yarn, fabric and clothing

21-26 microns – felting for garments

25-30 microns – socks, hats, scarves and felt

26-29 microns – knitting yarns, rugs, blankets, throws

Over 30 microns – bags, interior furnishings, carpets

Over 30 microns – felting, couch cushions, building insulation, stuffing

This list could go on and on but I just wanted to give you an idea of both the different uses and varying interpretation of microns.

From a hand spinner's point of view, provided the difference in microns is no more than three; and the difference in staple length (length of fibre) no more than an inch (2.5cms); then you shouldn't have any problem in mixing fibres, and making a really good yarn. In other words don't put a very fine fleece with a really coarse one. The coarse one will override the softness of the fine one.

The view of Mills for processing differs from mill to mill, and you would need to liaise with them as to what they find acceptable.

Whilst it isn't something that I do, many fleeces are mixed with wool/silk/nylon etc to change the effect of the alpaca fibre on whatever is being made. So, as an example, a coarse (high micron) may be mixed with something else to make it much softer or more elastic.

If you are heading in that direction and mixing fibres, please ensure you are aware of the labelling laws in your country with regard to yarn and anything else you make.

Currently under EU regulations you can mix alpaca with wool/silk/nylon etc and still call it 100% alpaca – provided that the alpaca element is no less than 70%.

However as rules frequently change, please do check first.

5 MICRONS AND THE BUYER

Many businesses will buy your fleeces either to sell on to someone else, or to add to their own fleeces for mill processing. In these instances it is most likely that you will be paid according to the microns. However, on the whole the buyer will be able to identify the micron so it isn't always necessary for you to have the fibre tested beforehand. However you should check with them first.

Comparatively, in sheep, I understand that in the UK the fleeces are sold as a whole at a fixed price by breed, to the British Wool Marketing Board. Therefore there is no need for micron testing to determine the price of the sheep fleece.

The usage of the micron value is one that is easily recognised by those who have alpacas. However, from my own experience, the general public would appear to be totally unaware of it. They therefore view the alpaca fleece or product by how soft it feels/looks, and what colour it is. As they don't know about microns, they rarely, if ever, ask.

Certainly, in all the years that I have sold fleeces and products, I have only once been asked what the micron value was. I confirmed that I had not had the fleece tested and therefore didn't know. The buyer however purchased the fleece from the photograph included in the advertisement, and went on to order different colour fleeces.

It is true to say that if you peruse some of the advertisements offering fleeces for sale, very rarely do you see the micron referred to.

So how do you know what the best use of the fibre is? For me, the best analogy is human hair. As a baby we have very fine downy hair which will not hold a plait. As we grow older the hair thickens but can still be a bit wispy. It will hold a plait but not tightly. The older we get and the hair becomes thicker and denser, the more likely it is that we can plait the hair and it will hold exactly how we plaited it. Past a certain age it gets less dense and the plait gets thinner.

Experienced hand and mill spinners know from the

look and feel of the fleece exactly what it can be used for – even if they have only seen a photograph.

6 SPINNING INTO YARN

Hand Spinning - By the time we decided to actually do something with the fleece we had two years supply and additional fleeces donated by friends (guess they didn't know what to do with it!).

I decided to learn how to spin and found a suitable class through a Spinners Guild. I made sure that my tutor was fully experienced and compassionate, for I was absolutely clueless about fibre of any description.

After the first day I was eager to throw the spinning wheel out of the window, and not return for a second class. But the tutor was compassionate (remember that was one of the qualifications I sought) and loaned me a spinning wheel to practice on at home. In the quietness of the house and without competition from other members of the group who were doing much better than I, it all became much easier. The determination and interest that I started with returned and having mastered the basic skill, I was able to sail through the rest of the course with ease.

That course taught me about skirting and washing sheep fleeces, carding (more about that later) working with wool, cotton, silk, recycled bottle tops, hemp, and even dog hair. I learned the difference between long draw and short draw and how to ply the yarn. I also learned about drop spindling but I have to admit that I wasn't very good at that. Luckily, at my request, we also played with an alpaca fleece that I proudly took in to class. As an aside you don't have to wash alpaca fleece which is going to be spun as it contains no lanolin. It will be washed after it is plied and made into a skein, in order to set the spinning.

If you think you would like to learn to spin then please do find someone from a Guild. At the one I used they would loan any equipment for you to use at home, so the only expense was enrolling for the class. The tutor provided all the materials and thankfully tea and coffee.

Mill Spinning – Armed with the newly gleaned knowledge I had gained from the Hand Spinning class, we sought out a local mill. Whilst there are many mills around that you can just send your fleeces to, as we were novices we wanted to have a one-to-one chat with the processor. This Mill also had a shop full of things that had been woven from sheep and alpaca and sometimes a mixture of both. There were scarves, cushions, throws, and garments, so we got lots of ideas as well as indication of price for a completed item.

We learned that you cannot use wool spun for weaving, to actually knit with, for it knits on the slant. I didn't believe him so tried it for myself and it was true. But, you can use yarn spun for knitting, also for weaving with no problem. Inspired by all the things in the shop, we decided that I would learn to weave and therefore we definitely needed the yarn spun for knitting. (Rather than the other way round). For weaving I had learned from the spinning class that we would need a 2 fold yarn (2 ply), but we also knew that not many knitters would use a 2ply although those who did crochet would. So, we also agreed to have 4ply. As alpaca fleece is much warmer than sheep, we decided against Double Knit.

We were disappointed to learn though that the finished product wouldn't be ready for several months and this seems to be true of all Mills. So you do need to get your fleeces to your chosen Mill as soon as possible.

The Mill gave us lots of choices, just washed and dried

fibre, carded fibre, picked fibre (just all pulled apart by machine – great for stuffing), coned yarn, hanks (skeins) or balls. As we were on a limited budget we chose the coned yarn. We have lived to regret it though sometimes, because winding from a cone into a ball even with equipment does take up time. But the upside is that it's easy to wind into skeins for dyeing into pretty colours.

7 DYEING FIBRE

Learning to hand dye became a necessary option for us. Whilst the Mill offered to have the yarn professionally dyed for us, this seemed an unnecessary expense.

Most of our fleeces were white but we do have many coloured alpacas too. We decided that we would hand dye some of the white and simply see what happened.

Hand dyeing is exciting, for you are never absolutely certain of the exact colour that will result. It does take quite a lot of time though for the whole process, but it is really worthwhile.

There are many types of dyes, and alpaca fibre takes up the dye quite well. For muted colours we have used natural dyes. For brighter colours we have used acid dyes. Brighter colour still is achieved by using Fibre Reactive dyes.

I don't intend in this book to go into the methods of dyeing. There are many good books already written on the subject as well as hoards of You-tube videos. My favourite book is, Color in Spinning by Deb Menz. It gives you guidance on spinning, dyeing, carding, and even items to make as well as lots of colour charts. It truly is a fantastic Spinners and Dyers Bible and one that I would not want to part with. There are, however, many other books to chose from – I just happen to think that this one covers most of the things I need to know.

Whilst you can dye your fleece before making into yarn, we were advised by the Mill we used that if we did that, they wouldn't be able to spin it for us – apparently it would damage their machines. But that was not a problem for we wanted to only dye part of our white fleeces once they had been made into beautiful yarn.

If, however, you are going to hand-spin then dyeing raw fibre isn't a problem. If you go in this direction then you can make beautiful textured yarns by blending several colours together in different formats.

But now that we had learned to dye we ventured into

learning to weave for this would add another way of selling the end results of our fibre. here.

8 WEAVING

Taking up this additional craft was just, for us, natural progression. We had so many cones of Alpaca yarn which we had made into skeins and balls. Some of the skeins we had already dyed and they were such beautiful colours. Whilst I knit and crochet, I wanted to be able to make something that was really light in weight and with unique colours.

I was fortunate that the tutor of the Spinning Class, was also the tutor for Weaving. I say 'fortunate' for I already knew that she was a very patient and compassionate person!

She provided a choice of looms to use and also provided all the other equipment needed, including a huge choice of yarns. The first day was fantastic and I was thrilled to be there. The looms were already set up with yarn and all I had to do was take the yarn through the 'shed' (the gap between two lines of yarn). It was just so easy, back and forth only having to change the 'shed' at the end of each row to make a pattern from the instructions provided. I was extremely proud of the very short scarf I made with its lovely pattern and two coloured yarns. Happy days!

The next tuition day though was completely different and this time the tutor started using what to me was a foreign language. We had migrated from the word 'shed' and opened up a completely new vocabulary. Words like 'warp/sett/reed/weft/shaft' entered the training and I had no idea what she was talking about. My brain was stunned and I felt sure I wouldn't be able to do this.

But, that night I sat and read The Big Book of Weaving by Laila Lundell. The help it offered was invaluable and in one reading I was able to not only understand the language, but was able to assimilate all the tutoring I been given that day.

After that, life in class was a breeze. I tried all sorts of yarns and patterns and finished the course with renewed confidence in my abilities.

Of course, armed with the new knowledge, we invested in a loom. There are many different types and sizes and much depends on the size of the space you have, and what sort of things you intend to make. I chose a collapsible table top loom which when folded takes up little room.

The world truly was our oyster after that, with money saved on Christmas presents as family members and friends all got given woven scarves!

Since then we have migrated to bigger and better scarves, wraps, stoles, throws, cushion covers and of course just fabric to cut and make into other things.

It is amazing that all of these things are a result of a fleece that has simply been carded making all the strands go in one direction so that it can be spun.

9 CARDING AND COMBING

Carding is a process which simply ensures that all the fibre ends up in a parallel state. You can use hand carders for this which look like a dog's brush although a lot larger. The product from hand-carding is called a 'rolag'. Hand-carding though is a long process and made my hands ache, so we eventually moved to a drum carder which means you can card a lot more fleece.

Drum-carders are easily used providing you tease or pick (pull apart) the fleece to start off with. The picking will of course loosen any dirt or organic matter that you didn't pull out prior to storing your fleeces. The more you pick – the more stuff will fall out so make sure you have something for this to fall onto – preferably not your own clothing! No matter how much preparation work you do, you can be sure that the drum-carder will find more dust and organic matter and this falls through a small slot onto your working surface.

If you are using a drum-carder this is a great time to start blending different colours together. You can use the natural colour fibre from your coloured fleeces or the fibre that you have hand dyed. Arranging the fibre in different orders will create different patterns. Do remember that what you see on the drum carder will be different once you have spun it!

My drum carder easily provides me with 50gm of fibre – called 'batts'. There are however much bigger drum-carders you can purchase or hire.

Combing is process using steel combs which are extremely sharp – do mind your fingers. Unlike carding, combing removes all short hairs usually caused by second cuts. You end up with two piles of fibre, one contains all the really good fibre (tops or slivers) in a long strand, and the other, fibre that has been combed out which you set aside to use for something else.

Again, with either of these processes you are learning a new language, but you do end up with your fibre processed suitable for spinning.

The book Color in Spinning mentioned before gives a step by step guide on all of these processes.

For the purpose of this book though, whether you have made rolags, batts, tops or slivers (or any other name used in different parts of the world), all are completely saleable. Lots of spinners do not want to have to do the preparatory work and in doing it for them you are providing a really good service and monetising your fleece.

The carded or combed fibre is also used for both dry and wet-felting which provides yet another market.

10 WET AND DRY (NEEDLE) FELTING

Felt fabric is a beautiful, tactile fabric that is easy to work with. It can be used for many different things from fun toys, decorations and stylish accessories for the home and to wear. For those of you who have washed a woollen jumper on the wrong temperature, you know how easy it is to felt a garment with overly hot water.

Wet Felting – It is outside the remit of this book to tell you how to felt but suffice it to say wet felting involves, water, soap and lots of elbow grease. The constant agitation of carded fibre laid out in a pattern of your choice provides the much needed felt.

Felt made in this way can be used for a multitude of things. You can mould it into shape for something like a hat, or simply keep it flat to use for making soft toys, decorations, cushion covers, throws etc or to be cut up for clothing.

Needle Felting – as it implies needle felting is done by constantly piercing your carded fibre (be careful of your fingers) with special barbed needles that interlock the fibres until they bond together. Very useful for embellishing items with decorative motives or jazzing up accessories for the home or clothing. Using a polystyrene base or an armature made from pipe cleaners or metal, you can make the most beautiful toys.

In the book Quick & Clever Felting by Ellen Kharade she shows you how to both wet and dry felt and provides lots of lovely ideas of what to do with your felt. It contains lots of easy to understand instructions.

Both methods will add value to your fibre and whatever you produce, and will help recoup the cost of your shearing.

Needle Felting in particular is a great way to use up odds and ends, particular for the bits that form the base of toys.

11 TOY MAKING AND STUFFING

Toys are very popular items to sell and whether you use your alpaca fibre to knit, crochet, or felt the toy, they will always need stuffing.

Whilst in most instances we will be using the blanket (1sts) for our garments and home accessories, when it comes to stuffing we use the 2nd grade. This comes from the neck, rump, legs and belly. In some countries the 2nd grade is further sub-divided so that neck and rump are classed as 2nd and legs and belly are classed as 3rd. As I don't separate these at shearing time, I refer to all of these bits as 2nd grade.

For stuffing you need to have washed and teased (picked) your fibre first. Remember in doing this we are pulling the fibre apart, not only does this remove any organic matter that remains, but it aerates the fibre. If you fail to tease your fibre, you will end up with lumps and bumps in your stuffing rather than a soft squidgy toy.

If you want to use your stuffing for much bigger items like cushions, and quilts then I would recommend using the needle felting technique at spaced intervals to stop the fibre bunching up with use or washing.

Teased too much stuffing? – Just put it out for the birds – they love to build their nests with it.

There are pieces of equipment you can purchase especially for picking. They are really useful if you want to prepare a large amount of fibre.

Personally I find it very therapeutic to do it by hand during those long drawn out winter nights.

But what if, you don't enjoy any crafts and having understood the need to increase its value, you want someone else to do it for you? Should you get another crafts person to do it for you?

12 CRAFTING V NOT CRAFTING

Without any doubt at all if you want a healthy return on your fleeces then you need to either learn a craft or pay someone else to do it for you.

Carding - Yes it does take time but it is worth it. You can sell carded fibre to spinners and felters. You can pay your local Mill to do it for you, but this will increase your own costs which will in turn increase the cost of your product.

Spinning - I found spinning difficult at first but now it's really easy and therapeutic. If you don't want to do it yourself, contact your local Guild who should be able to give you the name of lots of spinners eager to take on your job. Do find out though how much your chosen hand spinner will charge as you will need to factor this in. Having the fleece spun at the Mill increases the cost to you and should be taken into account with your costing.

Knitting and crochet – Whilst I have not touched on this subject, clearly your spun yarn can be used for knitting and crochet. If you are experienced in either of these fields then you will find no difficulty in adapting any pattern to suit the ply of your alpaca yarn. Alternatively, there are many people who enjoy this as a hobby and will take up your offer to make up your yarn into something you have chosen. There are no set rules for what their charges are, so do ask first.

There are a few businesses that are devising patterns for their yarn and selling the pattern with sufficient yarn to make the product. This is yet another monetising option.

Weaving – Once I understood the language, I found weaving really easy. It does take time to set up the loom but after that weaving is really quick, and produces lovely accessories for the home and clothing. It can also be used as cloth. Again, you could find someone to do this for you, or your local Mill may offer this service.

Dyeing – We added lots of choices to our buyers with the introduction of many different colours. I have no idea how much it costs to have this done professionally but certainly my local Mill would not spin fibre after it has been dyed.

Felting – There is so much you can do with felt whether it's wet felt or needle felt. You are spoilt for choice in what you can make.

All of the above will give more value to your fleeces but what if you simply just want to sell the fleece?

Selling Your Fleece - It's up to you whether you sell the blanket on its own or you sell it with the 2nd grade fibre (neck, rump, legs and belly). Either way you need to weigh it so your buyer knows what you are offering.

Many Spinning Guilds are happy to purchase your Alpaca Fleeces so that should be your first port of call. They will certainly pay you a lot more than many of the merchants who will buy your fleece and then sell it on. In many instances, the latter option may not cover your shearing costs.

You also have the choice of selling a whole fleece or selling in smaller packages i.e. 50gm, 100gm, 200gm and so on. This is a good way of introducing people to the joy of using Alpaca fleece.

In my case I didn't find a spinner who would buy my fleeces, because a member of the Spinning Guild was also an alpaca breeder and had sold their own fleeces to them. So what's the next option? I had to find other ways to let people know about my fleeces and products.

13 HOW AND WHERE TO SELL

How to market your Fleeces and resulting products is a book in itself, but here are some general tips which I hope you will find useful:-

Craft Fairs – there are a huge number of these taking place throughout the year. The cost of a stall varies but you can display not only your fleece but all of the resulting products. Take the time to display them nicely so that they look attractive. Put out raw fleeces showing their best attributes. Also list the weights of the fleece. If you have separated the blankets from the 2nds then give the weight of each and of course a price for the blanket and a lower price for the 2nds.

If you have made yarns, make sure you have nice professional looking labels that detail the weight of the yarn and that it is 100% alpaca (provided it is), you should also give the ply of the yarn. These rules apply whether you have made the yarn into balls or skeins (hanks)

Seasonal Fairs/Country Markets – there is a season for almost everything nowadays. Apart from the normal Christmas, New Year, Summer, Winter, Autumn, Spring there is also Mother's Day, Father's Day and all sorts of other 'Days'. There's cricket season, tennis season, golf season, football season and so on. These are all times that you can exploit with products made especially for this occasion.

Your Own Website - If you don't have one, then now is a good time to get one. There are so many free websites now on offer with instructions written in easy to understand English as opposed to technical language.

Social Media – Facebook – Build a Fan Page on Facebook – it costs nothing and you can advertise all of your alpaca things on it for free. If you have a website, then link your Fan Page to your Website.

Social Media – Twitter – Linkedin etc – are all good places to advertise your website or Facebook page.

Free and Fee paying sites – Ebay, Etsy, Ravelry, Gumtree, Preloved, Amazon, Folksy, Facebook pages for your area , local papers, free ads, the list is endless. But, be aware of any fees that you have to pay for this cost needs to be factored into your pricing.

Auction on Ebay – please don't make the mistake that I see many people making on ebay and starting an auction at 99pence. Not everyone will see your fleece and you may receive only a starting bid. Sadly many fleeces are being sold at the starting price of 99pence! After you have paid your Ebay and PayPal fees you have very little left and the fleece has been completely devalued. Always start an auction at the lowest price you are willing to accept bearing in mind your shearing costs. Remember, if you don't give your fleece or products any value, then neither will anyone else.

Commission based selling – approach your local craft, clothes, accessories etc shops. Many shops are happy to sell on a commission basis. The commission varies some as low as 10% and others as high as 100%. Try to negotiate a good rate – the higher the commission is, the higher priced your goods will be and the least likely to sell. Decide how much you want and the commission is added.

14 HOW MUCH CAN I CHARGE?

After "what can I do with this fleece" the next question is always 'How Much Can I Charge'?

I am afraid that there is no set rule and prices vary from area to area.

As a general rule for any craft work you need to calculate as follows:-

Material Costs + Labour Costs + Advertising Fees + General Overheads – this will give you your minimum base cost. (The amount that you must recoup, before you start to make a profit)

Labour Costs are probably the hardest to get to grips with, for we all work at different speeds and have varying years of experience. But including an hourly rate for your time and expertise is a must or you are really selling yourself short and only recouping the cost of materials.

Next you have to determine the profit so a mark-up of 100% would simply be to multiply your base cost figure by two. But that doesn't actually mean a 100% profit.

Using a £29 base cost as an example and a mark up of 150% would result in a price of £72.50 (29 x 2.5) and will result in an actual profit of 60%.

Next you need to look at what your competitors are not just charging, but successfully selling. Ebay is a good starting point by looking at SOLD listings. But be aware that things on Ebay often go for very low amounts. Then do google searches to 'buy Alpaca Scarf' that will throw up lots of sites that you can check on.

How you price your things is up to you – you can start high and if it doesn't sell then bring the price down. But never go too low for you devalue your product and yourself. I prefer to aim in the middle which gives me room to price up or down. People are prepared to pay good money for good products, sometimes it takes a little longer than others but it will happen, particularly as your reputation increases.

Without a doubt there is competition from people

desperate to sell their wares and of course the additional problem of imported goods. There are a few people already selling Alpaca products that they have imported and thereby using much lower pricing. It pays to ask them where the product was actually made if you think the price is much lower than you could reasonably charge yourself.

There is also the added competition from goods advertised as 100% Alpaca when in fact they have been blended with other wools/silk etc. Remember the EU labelling rules allow for this to happen legally.

Finally always remember the VAT man if you live in the UK, and other taxes if you live outside of the UK. It's likely if you are keeping Alpacas in the UK that you are also VAT registered. Fleeces, yarn, clothing (not for babies) hand made goods etc all carry 20% VAT. You definitely need to factor this VAT payment to HMRC when calculating your base cost.

15 IN CLOSING

I do hope that you can now see that there are so many different things you can do with your fleeces. What's more you can use every single bit of your fleece so that nothing is wasted.

If you are advertising on any of the sites I have mentioned, then good photographs are the key. They need to show your fleece or products off to their best advantage with a nice background that doesn't detract from what you are offering. Anything you write should express the wonders of what you are selling and pre-answer any questions the buyer might have.

Keywords (oh dear getting technical!) are words that people search on. You need to make sure these are in your listings. How do you know what the keywords are? A good place to start with is Ebay SOLD listings. Search for Alpaca and whatever your item is – so

'Alpaca Fleece' as an example. See what people are putting in their headings and mimic them – I said mimic not copy!

For whatever reason you are keeping Alpacas, they will always produce a fleece. Please don't store them in the barn – you have made your Alpaca give up its coat albeit for its benefit. But, now that you have it, please share its softness, its luxury, and its warmth with someone who can treasure it. After all items made from 100% Pure Alpaca are considered family heirlooms.

Don't be put off by the competition or lower prices. Clothing designers selling high priced items never got put off by the opening of Matalan or Primark! The value of your fleece rests with how you feel about your fleece and that will be reflected in your pricing.

In planning what to do with your fleece you truly are limited by your own imagination.

Enjoy, and treasure, your Alpacas and their fleeces!

Made in the USA
San Bernardino, CA
21 December 2017